THE ROYAL COURT THEATRE PRESENTS

Hole

by Ellie Kendrick

Hole is part of the Royal C...
supported by Jerwood Cha...

Hole was first performed...
Upstairs, Sloane Square,...

Hole
by Ellie Kendrick

CAST (in alphabetical order)

Ronke Adekoluejo
Ebony Bones
Alison Halstead
Rubyyy Jones
Cassie Layton
Eva Magyar

Directors **Helen Goalen, Abbi Greenland**
Designer **Cécile Trémolières**
Lighting Designer **Katharine Williams**
Composer **Ebony Bones**
Sound Designer **Emily Legg**
Casting Director **Lotte Hines CDG**
Production Manager **Marius Rønning**
Costume Supervisor **Ruth Best**
Stage Managers **Surenee Chan Somchit, Zo Elsmore**
Stage Management Work Placement **Melody Hui-Ling Lo**
Set built by **Royal Court Stage Department**

The Royal Court and Stage Management wish to thank the following for their help with this production:
Gwyneth Herbert, Alex McPherson.

Hole
by Ellie Kendrick

Ellie Kendrick (Writer)

Ellie's previous work at the Royal Court includes *Silly Girl* (part of The Big Idea programme). Other works developed at the Royal Court include *TABS*, which was in the top 10 for the 2015 Bruntwood Prize for Playwriting. She has taken part in three writing groups at the Royal Court, including an invitational group in 2016, during which this play was written. She is one of two Jerwood New Playwrights of 2018.

Ronke Adekoluejo (Ensemble)

For the Royal Court: **Bad Roads.**

Other theatre includes: **Cyprus Avenue (Abbey, Dublin/Public, NYC); The Mountaintop (Young Vic); Twelfth Night (Filter); The Oresteia (HOME, Manchester); Pride & Prejudice (Crucible, Sheffield); The House That Will Not Stand, The Colby Sisters of Pittsburgh Pennsylvania (Kiln); Anon (WNO); Random (Crooked Path).**

Television includes: **Faith, Cuckoo, Rough Cut, Doctor Who, NW, Cold Feet, Sick Note, Josh, Chewing Gum, Suspects, The Forgiving Earth.**

Film includes: **Christopher Robin, Been So Long, Ready Player One, One Crazy Thing, Lascivious Grace, Broken.**

Ruth Best (Costume Supervisor)

Dance includes: **Roma, III, The Gift (Salvatore Siciliano Ballet Company, Berlin).**

Opera includes: **Il trionfo del Tempo e del Disinganno (Kiez Oper, Berlin).**

Ebony Bones (Composer/Ensemble)

Ebony is a London-born composer, producer, singer and songwriter. Noted for her collaborations with Yoko Ono, Ebony has been enlisted by Yves Saint Laurent and Alexander Wang to score campaigns and runway shows. She first uploaded an anonymous demo to MySpace in 2008 entitled *We Know All About U*, which became the BBC's most played record by an unsigned artist.

In the time since, Ebony has released three full-length albums garnering widespread critical praise. Her most recent release *Nephilim* on her own label, 1984 Records, is a collaboration with the Beijing Philharmonic Orchestra, who perform her compositions.

Helen Goalen (Director)

Theatre for RashDash includes: **Three Sisters (Royal Exchange, Manchester/Tobacco Factory/Yard/ Cambridge Junction/MAYK/Bristol Old Vic); Snow White & Rose Red (Cambridge Junction/ BAC); The Darkest Corners (Transform Festival); Two Man Show (Northern Stage/Soho); We Want You To Watch (National); Oh, I Can't Be Bothered, The Frenzy, The Ugly Sisters, Set Fire To Everything (Lyric, Hammersmith/ Greenwich+Docklands International Festival/ Imagine Watford/Latitude Festival); Scary Gorgeous (Hull Truck/Theatre in the Mill, Bradford); Another Someone.**

Abbi Greenland (Director)

Theatre for RashDash includes: **Three Sisters (Royal Exchange, Manchester/Tobacco Factory/Yard/ Cambridge Junction/MAYK/Bristol Old Vic); Snow White & Rose Red (Cambridge Junction/ BAC); The Darkest Corners (Transform Festival); Two Man Show (Northern Stage/Soho); We Want You To Watch (National); Oh, I Can't Be Bothered, The Frenzy, The Ugly Sisters, Set Fire To Everything (Lyric, Hammersmith/ Greenwich+Docklands International Festival/ Imagine Watford/Latitude Festival); Scary Gorgeous (Hull Truck/Theatre in the Mill, Bradford); Another Someone.**

Alison Halstead (Ensemble)

Theatre includes: **Future Bodies (HOME, Manchester/RashDash/Unlimited); Julius Caesar (Sheffield Theatres); The House of Bernarda Alba (Graeae/Royal Exchange, Manchester); Blood Wedding (Graeae/Dundee Rep); Exhibit B (Barbican); Prometheus Awakes (Graeae/La Fura dels Baus); Macbeth, As You Like It, King John (Chicago Shakespeare); Antigone, No Place Like Home (Steppenwolf); Aida (ENO); Wondrous Strange (Mimbre/RSC); Falling Up (Mimbre/National).**

Lotte Hines CDG (Casting Director)

For the Royal Court: **Pests (& Clean Break).**

Other theatre includes: **The Wolves (Theatre Royal, Stratford East); Things of Dry Hours, La Musica, Dirty Butterfly, The Island (Young Vic); Meek, Junkyard, Boys Will Be Boys, The Glass Menagerie, People Places & Things (& National/UK tour), The Absence of War, Medea (Headlong); As You Like It, Pride & Prejudice, To Kill a Mockingbird (Regent's Park Open Air); The Barbershop Chronicles (& National/Fuel/US tour), The Crucible (Leeds Playhouse); Elephant (Birmingham Rep); Speech & Debate (Trafalgar**

Studios); Brenda (& HighTide Festival), Removal Men (Yard); The Illiad, The Weir (Lyceum, Edinburgh); Pride & Prejudice (Crucible, Sheffield); The Boy in the Striped Pyjamas (Chichester Festival); Another Place (Theatre Royal, Plymouth); We Are Proud to Present... (Bush); The Little Mermaid (Bristol Old Vic); Pieces of Vincent (Arcola).

Film includes: CLA'AM (short), Above (short).

As casting associate, other theatre includes: Harry Potter & the Cursed Child (West End); The Seagull (Regent's Park Open Air); Tipping the Velvet (Lyric, Hammersmith/Lyceum, Edinburgh); Bull (Crucible, Sheffield).

As casting assistant, other theatre includes: Hamlet (Barbican/West End); A View from the Bridge (Young Vic).

Lotte worked as Casting Associate for the Royal Court from 2008–2012 and then as Deputy Casting Director from 2012- 2014.

Rubyyy Jones (Ensemble)

Theatre includes: Corpus Christi, A Midsummer Night's Dream (Arcola); Taylor Mac (Barbican); Long Live Queen James (Hampton Court Palace/ Banqueting House).

Solo shows include: HIDDEN WOMYYYN, RAAAGE (VAULT Festival).

As headline/featured/solo artist, events include: Queer & Now (V&A); Copenhagen International Performance Art Festival; Vienna Queer Performance Festival; Pride Programme (Brussels/Tel Aviv/London/Slovenia/ Manchester/Oxford/Berlin/Florence).

Awards include: Burlesque Hall of Fame Award for 'Most Innovative'.

Cassie Layton (Ensemble)

Theatre includes: Secret Theatre (Sam Wanamaker Playhouse); Persuasion (Royal Exchange, Manchester); Macbeth (Young Vic); Romeo & Juliet (Globe); Pitcairn (Chichester Festival/Out of Joint); Sense & Sensibility (Watermill).

Television includes: Father Brown, Holby City, Doctors, The Commoners, Lovesick, Saturdays.

Film includes: Pylon, Jarhead 2, #Iamthescariest (short), La Petite Mort (short).

Radio includes: The Quanderhorn Xperimentations, Home Front, Cassandra at the Wedding, Pilgrim, Chiwawa, Clayton Grange, The Pursued, Plain Murder, The Cazalets, Dog Days, The Interplanetary Notes of Ambassador B, The Divine Comedy, What Would Elizabeth Bennett Do?, The Rivals.

Emily Legg (Sound Designer)

For the Royal Court: Katzenmusik, Road [as associate], Plaques & Tangles, Young Court Season, Live Lunch, The Get Out, Gastronauts, Lost in Theatre (Open Court).

Other theatre includes: Turning a Little Further (Young Vic); Checkpoint 22 (New Diorama/ Edinburgh Festival Underbelly); Pedro Peramo is My Father (Elan Frantolo).

Emily is Deputy Head of Sound at the Royal Court and produces the Royal Court Playwright's Podcast.

Eva Magyar (Ensemble)

Theatre includes: Tristan & Yseult, Hedda Gabler, From Morning to Midnight (National); The Cherry Orchard (Bristol Old Vic/Royal Exchange, Manchester); Marlene (Soho); 12 Proposals for a Better Europe (Belarus/Leeds Playhouse); The Wild Bride, Midnight's Pumpkin (Kneehigh).

Television includes: Father Brown, X Company, Paranoid, Mars, Hollyoaks.

Film includes: Overlord, X-Men: First Class, Monte Carlo, Rogue One: A Star Wars Story, Let Me Go, Darkwoods, Headhunter.

Cécile Trémolières (Designer)

As design assistant, for the Royal Court: Grimly Handsome.

As designer, other theatre includes: Midsummer, 306 (National Theatre of Scotland); Kevin, Portrait d'un apprenti converti (Théâtre National de Bretagne/Théâtre des Quartiers d'Ivry); Mayfly (Orange Tree); Porcelain (Abbey, Dublin); The Tide (Young Vic); Suzy Storck, The Iphigenia Quartet (Gate); This Beautiful Future, The Mikvah Project (Yard); Punkplay (Southwark); My People (Clwyd); Invisible Treasure (Ovalhouse).

As designer, opera includes: Il Trionfo (Alte Münze, Berlin); Madama Butterfly [costume] (Arcola); La Tragédie de Carmen [set] (Wilton's Music Hall/ROH).

Awards include: European Opera Directing Prize Award.

Cécile's work has been exhibited at the Prague Quadrennial, the V&A exhibition Make/Believe: UK Design for Performance and at the World Stage Design exhibition in Taipei.

Katharine Williams (Lighting Designer)

For the Royal Court: **Men in the Cities, Not I, The Westbridge.**

Other theatre includes: **Two Man Show, The Darkest Corners (RashDash); Gagarin Way (Dundee Rep); Women in Power (Nuffield, Southampton); All of Me, Status (China Plate); Education, Education, Education (Wardrobe Ensemble); Flood – Part Four (SlungLow); Instructions for Border Crossing, Going Viral, Error 404 (Daniel Bye); Big Guns (Yard); Medea (Bristol Old Vic); An Injury (Permanent Red); Am I Dead Yet?, You Have Been Upgraded, The Noise (Unlimited); Ode to Leeds (Leeds Playhouse); The Croydon Avengers (Harrogate); The Rivals (Watermill); The Department of Distractions, Partus (Third Angel); Dealer's Choice (Royal & Derngate, Northampton); Dolls (National Theatre of Scotland).**

Dance includes: **Faeries (ROH); Underdrome (Roundhouse); Outre (South Bank); I Am Falling (Gate/Sadler's Wells).**

Opera includes: **Adriano in Syria (Britten); The Faerie Queene (Middle Temple Hall); Bluebeard (Ovideu Opera House); Death Actually (Toynbee Hall); The Rape of Lucretia (Aldeburgh).**

Film includes: **I lit the Half-Light.**

Music & concerts include: **The Pleasure Garden, The Ring, The Lodger, Downhill, Champagne (BFI Hitchcock Season); Resonance at the Still Point of Change (South Bank); The Butterly Effect (Hong Kong Festival).**

As writer, theatre includes: **Walk with Me (VAULT Festival).**

Katharine was lead artist on the *Love Letters to the Home Office* project and the founder of Crew for Calais. She worked as documentary filmmaker on Clare Duffy's *Extreme Light North* project in Shetland and Canada.

THE ROYAL COURT THEATRE

The Royal Court Theatre is the writers' theatre. It is a leading force in world theatre for energetically cultivating writers – undiscovered, emerging and established.

Through the writers, the Royal Court is at the forefront of creating restless, alert, provocative theatre about now. We open our doors to the unheard voices and free thinkers that, through their writing, change our way of seeing.

Over 120,000 people visit the Royal Court in Sloane Square, London, each year and many thousands more see our work elsewhere through transfers to the West End and New York, UK and international tours, digital platforms, our residencies across London, and our site-specific work. Through all our work we strive to inspire audiences and influence future writers with radical thinking and provocative discussion.

The Royal Court's extensive development activity encompasses a diverse range of writers and artists and includes an ongoing programme of writers' attachments, readings, workshops and playwriting groups. Twenty years of the International Department's pioneering work around the world means the Royal Court has relationships with writers on every continent.

Within the past sixty years, John Osborne, Samuel Beckett, Arnold Wesker, Ann Jellicoe, Howard Brenton and David Hare have started their careers at the Court.
Many others including Caryl Churchill, Athol Fugard, Mark Ravenhill, Simon Stephens, debbie tucker green, Sarah Kane – and, more recently, Lucy Kirkwood, Nick Payne, Penelope Skinner and Alistair McDowall – have followed.

The Royal Court has produced many iconic plays from Lucy Kirkwood's **The Children** to Jez Butterworth's **Jerusalem** and Martin McDonagh's **Hangmen**.

Royal Court plays from every decade are now performed on stage and taught in classrooms and universities across the globe.

It is because of this commitment to the writer that we believe there is no more important theatre in the world than the Royal Court.

Supported using public funding by
ARTS COUNCIL ENGLAND

JERWOOD CHARITABLE FOUNDATION

Jerwood New Playwrights is a longstanding partnership between Jerwood Charitable Foundation and the Royal Court. Each year, Jerwood New Playwrights supports the production of two new works by emerging writers, all of whom are in the first 10 years of their career.

The Royal Court carefully identifies playwrights whose careers would benefit from the challenge and profile of being fully produced either in the Jerwood Downstairs or Jerwood Upstairs Theatres at the Royal Court.

Since 1994, the programme has produced a collection of challenging and outspoken works which explore a variety of new forms and voices and so far has supported the production of 85 new plays. These plays include: Joe Penhall's **Some Voices**, Nick Grosso's **Peaches** and **Real Classy Affair**, Judy Upton's **Ashes and Sand**, Sarah Kane's **Blasted, Cleansed** and **4.48 Psychosis**, Michael Wynne's **The Knocky** and **The People Are Friendly**, Judith Johnson's **Uganda**, Sebastian Barry's **The Steward of Christendom**, Jez Butterworth's **Mojo**, Mark Ravenhill's **Shopping and Fucking**, Ayub Khan Din's **East Is East** and **Notes on Falling Leaves**, Martin McDonagh's **The Beauty Queen of Leenane**, Jess Walters' **Cockroach, Who?**, Tamantha Hammerschlag's **Backpay**, Connor McPherson's **The Weir**, Meredith Oakes' **Faith**, Rebecca Prichard's **Fair Game**, Roy Williams' **Lift Off, Clubland** and **Fallout**, Richard Bean's **Toast** and **Under the Whaleback**, Gary Mitchell's **Trust** and **The Force of Change**, Mick Mahoney's **Sacred Heart** and **Food Chain**, Marina Carr's **On Raftery's Hill**, David Eldridge's **Under the Blue Sky** and **Incomplete and Random Acts of Kindness**, David Harrower's **Presence**, Simon Stephens' **Herons, Country Music** and **Motortown**, Leo Butler's **Redundant** and **Lucky Dog**, Enda Walsh's **Bedbound**, David Greig's **Outlying Islands**, Zinnie Harris' **Nightingale and Chase**, Grae Cleugh's **Fucking Games**, Rona Munro's **Iron**, Ché Walker's **Fleshwound**, Laura Wade's **Breathing Corpses**, debbie tucker green's **Stoning Mary**, Gregory Burke's **On Tour**, Stella Feehily's **O Go My Man**, Simon Faquhar's **Rainbow Kiss**, April de Angelis, Stella Feehily, Tanika Gupta, Chloe Moss and Laura Wade's **Catch**, Polly Stenham's **That Face** and **Tusk Tusk**, Mike Bartlett's **My Child**, Fiona Evans' **Scarborough**, Levi David Addai's **Oxford Street**, Bola Agbaje's **Gone Too Far!** and **Off the Endz**, Alexi Kaye Campbell's **The Pride**, Alia Bano's **Shades**, Tim Crouch's **The Author**, DC Moore's **The Empire**, Anya Reiss' **Spur of the Moment** and **The Acid Test**, Penelope Skinner's **The Village Bike**, Rachel De-lahay's **The Westbridge** and **Routes**, Nick Payne's **Constellations**, Vivienne Franzmann's **The Witness** and **Pests**, E. V. Crowe's **Hero**, Anders Lustgarten's **If You Don't Let Us Dream, We Won't Let You Sleep**, Suhayla El-Bushra's **Pigeons**, Clare Lizzimore's **Mint**, Alistair McDowall's **Talk Show**, Rory Mullarkey's **The Wolf from the Door**, Molly Davies' **God Bless the Child**, Diana Nneka Atuona's **Liberian Girl**, Cordelia Lynn's **Lela & Co**, Nicola Wilson's **Plaques and Tangles**, Stef Smith's **Human Animals**, Charlene James' **Cuttin' It**, Nathaniel Martello-White's **Torn**, Alice Birch's **Anatomy of a Suicide**, Chris Thorpe's **Victory Condition** and Simon Longman's **Gundog**.

Jerwood Charitable Foundation is dedicated to imaginative and responsible revenue funding of the arts, supporting artists to develop and grow at important stages in their careers. It works with artists across art forms, from dance and theatre to literature, music and the visual arts.

jerwoodcharitablefoundation.org

ROYAL

COMING UP AT THE ROYAL COURT

5 Dec - 26 Jan

The Cane
By Mark Ravenhill

30 Jan - 16 Feb

Superhoe
By Nicôle Lecky
Talawa Theatre Company and Royal Court Theatre.

4 Feb – 16 Mar

Cyprus Avenue
By David Ireland
Abbey Theatre and Royal Court Theatre.

27 Feb - 23 Mar

Inside Bitch
Conceived by Stacey Gregg
& Deborah Pearson
Devised by Lucy Edkins,
Jennifer Joseph, TerriAnn Oudjar
and Jade Small.
Clean Break and Royal Court Theatre.

3 - 27 Apr

Pah-La
By Abhishek Majumdar

10 May - 15 Jun

White Pearl
By Anchuli Felicia King

14 May - 1 Jun

salt.
By Selina Thompson
Commissioned by MAYK, Theatre Bristol and Yorkshire

27 Jun - 10 Aug

the end of history
By Jack Thorne

4 -27 Jul

seven methods of
killing kylie jenne
By Jasmine Lee-Jones

royalcourttheatre.com

Sloane Square London, SW1W 8AS ⊖ Sloane Square
⇌ Victoria Station 🐦 royalcourt 🗗 royalcourttheatre

Supported using public fu
ARTS COU
ENGLAND

COURT

OYAL COURT SUPPORTERS

e Royal Court is a registered charity and not-for-profit mpany. We need to raise £1.5 million every year in dition to our core grant from the Arts Council and our ket income to achieve what we do.

e have significant and longstanding relationships with any generous organisations and individuals who provide al support. Royal Court supporters enable us to main the writers' theatre, find stories from everywhere d create theatre for everyone.

e can't do it without you.

INDIVIDUAL SUPPORTERS

Artistic Director's Circle
Eric Abraham
Carolyn Bennett
Samantha & Richard
  Campbell-Breeden
Cas Donald
Jane Featherstone
Lydia & Manfred Gorvy
Jean & David Grier
Charles Holloway
Luke Johnson
Jack & Linda Keenan
Mandeep & Sarah Manku
Anatol Orient
NoraLee & Jon Sedmak
Deborah Shaw
  & Stephen Marquardt
Matthew & Sian Westerman
Mahdi Yahya

Writers' Circle
Chris & Alison Cabot
Jordan Cook & John Burbank
Scott M. Delman
Virginia Finegold
Michelle & Jan Hagemeier
Chris Hogbin
Mark Kelly & Margaret
  McDonald Kelly
Nicola Kerr
Emma O'Donoghue
Tracy Phillips
Suzanne Pirret
Theo & Barbara Priovolos
Sir Paul & Lady Ruddock
Carol Sellars
Maria Sukkar
Jan & Michael Topham
Maureen & Tony Wheeler
Anonymous

Directors' Circle
Mrs Asli Arah
Dr Kate Best
Katie Bradford
Piers Butler
Sir Trevor & Lady Chinn
Joachim Fleury
David & Julie Frusher
Julian & Ana Garel-Jones
Louis Greig
David & Claudia Harding
Dr Timothy Hyde
Roderick & Elizabeth Jack
Mrs Joan Kingsley
Victoria Leggett
Emma Marsh
Rachel Mason
Andrew & Ariana Rodger
Simon Tuttle
Anonymous

Platinum Members
Simon A Aldridge
Moira Andreae
Nick Archdale
Clive & Helena Butler
Gavin & Lesley Casey
Sarah & Philippe Chappatte
Andrea & Anthony Coombs
Clyde Cooper
Victoria Corcoran
Mrs Lara Cross
Andrew & Amanda Cryer
Shane & Catherine Cullinane
Matthew Dean
Sarah Denning
Cherry & Rob Dickins
The Drabble Family
Denise & Randolph Dumas
Robyn Durie
Mark & Sarah Evans
Sally & Giles Everist
Celeste Fenichel
Emily Fletcher
The Edwin Fox Foundation
Dominic & Claire Freemantle
Beverley Gee
Paul & Kay Goswell
Nick & Julie Gould
The Richard Grand Foundation
Jill Hackel & Andrzej Zarzycki
Carol Hall
Sam & Caroline Haubold
Mr & Mrs Gordon Holmes
Soyar Hophinson
Damien Hyland
Amanda & Chris Jennings
Ralph Kanter
Jim & Wendy Karp
David P Kaskel
  & Christopher A Teano
Vincent & Amanda Keaveny
Peter & Maria Kellner
Mr & Mrs Pawel Kisielewski
Rosemary Leith
Mark & Sophie Lewisohn
Kathryn Ludlow
The Maplescombe Trust
Christopher Marek
  Rencki
Frederic Marguerre
Mrs Janet Martin
Andrew McIver
David & Elizabeth Miles
Jameson & Lauren Miller
Barbara Minto
M.E. Murphy Altschuler
Siobhan Murphy
Peter & Maggie Murray-Smith
Sarah Muscat
Liv Nilssen
Georgia Oetker
Andrea & Hilary Ponti
Greg & Karen Reid
Nick & Annie Reid

Paul & Gill Robinson
Corinne Rooney
William & Hilary Russell
Sally & Anthony Salz
Anita Scott
Bhags Sharma
Dr. Wendy Sigle
Andy Simpkin
Paul & Rita Skinner
Brian Smith
John Soler & Meg Morrison
Kim Taylor-Smith
Mrs Caroline Thomas
Alex Timken
The Ulrich Family
Monica B Voldstad
Arrelle & François Von Hurter
Mr N C Wiggins
Anne-Marie Williams
Sir Robert & Lady Wilson
Anonymous

With thanks to our Friends, Silver and Gold Members whose support we greatly appreciate.

DEVELOPMENT COUNCIL
Piers Butler
Chris Cabot
Cas Donald
Sally Everist
Celeste Fenichel
Tim Hincks
Emma Marsh
Anatol Orient
Andrew Rodger
Sian Westerman

Our Supporters contribute to all aspects of the Royal Court's work including: productions, commissions, writers' groups, International, Young Court, creative posts, the Trainee scheme and access initiatives as well as providing in-kind support.

For more information or to become a Supporter please contact Charlotte Cole: charlottecole@royalcourttheatre.com/020 7565 5049.

ROYAL

ASSISTED PERFORMANCES

Captioned Performances

Captioned performances are accessible for deaf, deafened & hard of hearing people as well as being suitable for people for whom English is not a first language.

In the Jerwood Theatre Downstairs
The Cane: Tue 8 Jan, 7.30pm & Fri 18 Jan, 7.30pm
Cyprus Avenue: Tue 12 Mar, 7.30pm
White Pearl: Wed 22 & 29 May, 5 & 12 Jun, 7.30pm
the end of history...: Wed 10, 17, 24, 31 Jul & 7 Aug 7.30pm

In the Jerwood Theatre Upstairs
Hole: Wed 2 Jan, 7.45pm
Inside Bitch: Wed 20 March, 7.45pm
Pah-La: Wed 24 April, 7.45pm
salt.: Fri 31 May, 7.45pm
seven methods of killing kylie jenner: Fri 19 Jul, 7.45pm

Audio Described Performances

Audio described performances are accessible for blind or partially sighted customers. They are preceded by a touch tour (at 1pm) which allows patrons access to elements of theatre design including set & costume.

In the Jerwood Theatre Downstairs
The Cane: Sat 19 Jan, 2.30pm
Cyprus Avenue: Sat 9 March, 2.30pm
White Pearl: Sat 8 June, 2.30pm
the end of history...: Sat 3 Aug, 2.30pm

COURT

ROYAL

ASSISTED PERFORMANCES

Performances in a Relaxed Environment

Relaxed Environment performances are suitable for those who may benefit from a more relaxed experience.

During these performances:

- There will be a relaxed attitude to noise in the auditorium; you are welcome to respond to the show in whatever way feels natural
- You can enter and exit the auditorium when needed
- We will help you find the best seats
- House lights remained raised slightly

The Cane: Mon 14 Jan, 7.30pm
Inside Bitch: Sat 23 Mar, 3pm
salt.: Sat 25 May, 7.45pm
White Pearl: Sat 1 Jun, 2.30pm
end of history...: Sat 27 Jul, 2.30pm

If you would like to talk to us about your access requirements please contact our Box Office at (0)20 7565 5000 or **boxoffice@royalcourttheatre.com.**
A Royal Court Visual Story is available on our website. We also produce a Story Synopsis & Sensory Synopsis which are available on request.

For more information and to book access tickets online, visit

royalcourttheatre.com/assisted-performances

Sloane Square London, SW1W 8AS ⊖ Sloane Square ⇄ Victoria Station
🐦 royalcourt 🅵 royalcourttheatre

ROYAL

BAR & KITCHEN

The Royal Court's Bar & Kitchen aims to create a welcoming and inspiring environment with a style and ethos that reflects the work we put on stage. Our menu, created by Head Chef David Adams, consists of simple, ingredient driven and flavour-focused dishes with an emphasis on freshness and seasonality. This is supported by a carefully curated drinks list notable for its excellent wine selection, craft beers and skilfully prepared coffee. By day a perfect spot for long lunches, meetings or quiet reflection and by night an atmospheric, vibrant meeting space for cast, crew, audiences and the general public.

GENERAL OPENING HOURS
Monday – Friday: 10am – late
Saturday: 12noon – late

Advance booking is suggested at peak times.

For more information and to book access tickets online, visit

royalcourttheatre.com/bar

HIRES & EVENTS

The Royal Court is available to hire for celebrations, rehearsals, meetings, filming, ceremonies and much more. Our two theatre spaces can be hired for conferences and showcases, and the building is a unique venue for bespoke weddings and receptions.

For more information and to book access tickets online, visit

royalcourttheatre.com/events

Sloane Square London, SW1W 8AS ⊖ Sloane Square ⇌ Victoria Station
🐦 royalcourt 🄵 royalcourttheatre

COURT

"There are no spaces, no rooms in my opinion, with a greater legacy of fearlessness, truth and clarity than this space."
Simon Stephens, Associate Playwright

The Royal Court invests in the future of the theatre, offering writers the support, time and resources to find their voices and tell their stories, asking the big questions and responding to the issues of the moment.

As a registered charity, the Royal Court needs to raise at least £1.5 million every year in addition to our Arts Council funding and ticket income, to keep seeking out, developing and nurturing new voices. Please join us by donating today.

You can donate online at **royalcourttheatre.com/donate** or via our **donation box in the Bar & Kitchen.**

We can't do it without you.

Support the Court

To find out more about the different ways in which you can be involved please contact Charlotte Cole on 020 7565 5049 / charlottecole@royalcourttheatre.com

The English Stage Company at the Royal Court Theatre is a registered charity (No. 231242).

HOLE

Ellie Kendrick

HOLE

OBERON BOOKS
LONDON

WWW.OBERONBOOKS.COM

First published in 2018 by Oberon Books Ltd
521 Caledonian Road, London N7 9RH
Tel: +44 (0) 20 7607 3637 / Fax: +44 (0) 20 7607 3629
e-mail: info@oberonbooks.com
www.oberonbooks.com

PB ISBN: 9781786825377
E ISBN: 9781786825384

Printed and bound by 4EDGE Limited, Hockley, Essex, UK.
eBook conversion by Lapiz Digital Services, India.

Visit www.oberonbooks.com to read more about all our books and to buy them.
You will also find features, author interviews and news of any author events, and
you can sign up for e-newsletters so that you're always first to hear about our new
releases.

Printed on FSC accredited paper

10 9 8 7 6 5 4 3 2 1

Notes

The word "Big" can mean any number of things. This might mean people who occupy their bodies in space in a way that feels radical and powerful, whatever that way is.

"Blackbody" is a phrase used in Physics to describe a theoretical object that can absorb all radiation.

"Singularity": in Physics, this word refers to a point in an equation that reaches an infinite number – sometimes a sign of a missing piece in the equation. In Astrophysics, singularities are points of infinite density according to the theory of general relativity. They are thought to exist at the centre of black holes.

This text is neither a series of instructions nor a poem.

The number of actors on stage doesn't necessarily have to be limited to those numbered in the text.

Under no circumstances should fat suits be used.

Thanks

E V Crowe, Lucy Morrison and the 'undeniable' writers on the Royal Court writing group on which this was written in Spring-Summer 2016. Abbi Greenland and Helen Goalen. Ikenna Obiekwe. Elizabeth Gibney. Layo-Christina Akinlude, Sheila Atim, Rachel Redford, Siobhán McSweeney and Susan Wokoma.

Darkness.
A voice:

VOICE:
I need you to listen. I need to tell you or I am going to
implode.

>*A spotlight snaps on.*
>*WOMAN 1 is lowered into the spotlight.*
>
>*She smiles. She speaks into the microphone – her mouth moves –*
>*"hello" – but we don't hear it.*
>*She leans forward into the microphone.*

WOMAN 1:
No no I can –

>*A timer starts: Tick. Tock.*
>*She points to the microphone enquiringly. The timer carries on*
>*ticking. Pause.*

I was swimming. I'm a swimmer!

>*Beat.*

That was inaccurate. Sorry.

>*Beat.*

I'm a professor. Astrophysics. I can tell you about singularities.

>*Beat.*

No – alright – what about stars?

>*Beat.*

Or – or – no what about a supernova – that's this massive
explosion before the star collapses into a supermassive
black h–

>*Beat.*

I'm so sorry, is this releva-(nt)?

Beat.

I'm sorry. I'm not understanding.

Silence. She looks around.

I'm happy – I'm happy to not. Whatever's –

Beat. She takes a deep breath.

I am trying to be helpful but I don't remember as much as I would like –

The microphone cuts out. She tries again.

I am trying to be helpful but I don't remember –

The microphone cuts out. She stops. Tries again.

I am trying to be helpful –

Cuts out.

I am trying to be –

Cuts out.

I am trying –

Cuts.

I am –

A 'WRONG' buzzer.
A hole opens up beneath her. She disappears into it. The spotlight snaps off.

* * *

Spotlight snaps on.
WOMAN 2 is lowered into the spotlight.
The timer starts. Tick, tock.

WOMAN 2:
I'm walking down the street at night and it's dark and there's
a man –

> *The spotlight moves away. She runs back into it. It narrows.*

I am walking down the street at night and it's dark –

> *The spotlight moves away again. She runs back into it. It narrows*
> *again.*

I am walking down the street at night –

> *The spotlight moves away again. She runs back into it. It narrows*
> *again. Now she has to kneel.*

I am walking down the street –

> *Again. Now she has to crouch.*

I am walking –

> *Again. Now just her head, pressed to the floor.*

I am –

> *The spotlight narrows to a tiny pool of light –*

I –

> *'WRONG' buzzer.*
> *The hole opens up. She disappears.*
> *Spotlight snaps off.*

* * *

Spotlight snaps on.
WOMAN 3 is lowered down.
Tick, tock.

WOMAN 3:
Okay so there's this woman that is so ugly that just looking at her will turn you to stone. Because she got raped by the guy who a goddess fancied. No – wait –

> *A big squelchy tomato falls on WOMAN 3's head from above. She continues.*

Okay there's this woman that is so ugly that just looking at her will turn you to stone. Because she got raped. No no –

> *Another tomato falls onto her head. She perseveres.*

Okay there's this woman who is so ugly that just looking at her will turn you to stone.

> *Splat. More tomatoes this time. Pelted. She wipes her face clean.*

Okay there's this woman who is so ugly that just looking at her –

> *Splat! More.*

Okay okay okay there's this woman who is so ugly –

> *SPLAT.*

Okay okay there's this woman –

> *S P L A T.*

Okay there's –

> *S S S P P P L L L A A A T T T*

Okay –

> *BUZZER.*

A MONSOON OF TOMATOES sweeps WOMAN 3 down into the hatch.

* * *

Spotlight comes on again.
WOMAN 4 is lowered into it.
She lies down.
Tick, tock.
She shrugs.

WOMAN 4:
I don't like standing up.

> *Buzzer. Down she goes.*

* * *

Spotlight comes on again.
WOMAN 5 is lowered into the spotlight.
Nothing. Silence. No tick tock.

WOMAN 5:
Would you mind if I just had something to –

> *A huge bottle of coke falls from above. She smiles warmly.*

Thank you so much.

> *She picks it up. Twinkles.*

I'm all about yes.

> *She opens the bottle and it erupts, fizzing all over her. She glugs at it to stop it spilling.*

Yes, yes, yes.

> *She pauses. Nothing happens. She glugs more of the coke. Wipes her mouth.*

Yes, yes, yes yes.

She glugs more and more.

Yesyesyesyesyesyesyesyesyesyesyes.

She glugs and glugs and glugs. Still nothing.

All about yes.

Nothing
Then
The spotlight narrows

No please

it narrows further

no

BUZZER. Hole opens. Gone.

Darkness.

The hatch in the floor starts to open.

A WOMAN pushes up out of the ground through the hatch dripping wet and covered in something sludgy.

She drags herself up as best she can. The spotlight snaps back onto her.

She tries to crawl out of the spotlight.

It follows her.

The spotlight increases in intensity.

She's trying to escape the spotlight. It's following her.

She stops. The spotlight follows her back to the hatch.

She looks up at the light –

She lowers herself back down the hatch.

CLANG. A weight falls onto the hatch, slamming it closed.

After a moment, her hands push up against the hatch again from beneath.

The spotlight shines on the hatch.

CLANG. An even bigger weight falls onto the hatch.

The spotlight shines on the closed hatch.

She bangs at the hatch.

Spotlight still on the hatch.

She keeps trying to bang against the hatch from underneath. The hatch doesn't budge.

She's still banging. She won't stop.

She stops.

Spotlight holds.

Spotlight drifts away from the hole then quickly snaps back again.

Spotlight holds.

Spotlight switches off.

Darkness. Still.

The squelchy sound of eating.

The air feels wet and close.

A rumbling from below.

a sound starts to infect the space

the sound is a far off growl

the growl is getting louder

BOOM.

What was that?

The ground starts to shake.

Something is coming up from below.

BANG. The ground shakes. It's still pitch black.

Strange wordless song begins to seep out from beneath the hatch

BANG. It shakes again.

The wordless song is overflowing into something terrifying

Now the ground starts to shake continually

BANG. BANG. BANG. It's like an earthquake. Bits of rubble and dust fall from the ceiling.

BANG. BANG. A fist punches up out through the hatch, illuminated from below.

BANG. Another fist.

The pair of fists pull down and

BANG – punch up again. A hole in the middle of the stage. A light shining up from the hole to the ceiling. The song spilling out from the hole.

BANG. The fists again. The hole gets bigger.

BANG. The hands reappear.

Someone is dragging themselves out of the hole

It's a woman. It's a Big Woman. She is singing. She is covered in dust. She is carrying a light attached to a cord. She hooks the light up. It momentarily blinds us.

She looks at us.

She puts a hand down the hole.

Another hand grabs it from below.

Another Big Woman pulls herself out of the hole. She is singing. She's carrying a big black box. She puts it down.

She looks at us too.

The second Big Woman puts her hand down the hole.

Another hand grabs it from below.

A third Big Woman pulls herself up. She is singing.

The song ends.

Silence.

They all look at us. They each pick up a tomato from the ground.

They hold out their tomatoes. They bring them to their mouths.

They mash the tomatoes between their strong palms.

They eat the mash.

They lick their hands.

They swallow.

They smile wide.

They're ready to start.

They look right at us.

1: We are big. We take up space.

There is more of us than you.

We mean physically.

We've got more cells.

We're growing.

We're growing right now.

We're producing thousands of cells every minute.

We're filling up the world with all our cells.

We're getting bigger.

We're getting wider.

We're gaining weight.

We're eating.

We're consuming.

1, 2, 3: We won't stop.

1: Your structures cannot hold me.

2: She breaks them with her body.

1: She means materially.

I break chairs.

1, 2, 3: We like it that way.

2: You can't handle me.

1: You can't handle us when we grow bigger.

2: She means literally.

You can't get your hands around me

1, 2, 3: We like it that way.

1: We have hands.

2: We have fists.

3: We have feet.

1: We have glands

2: We have flesh.

1, 2, 3: We eat wheat.

2: We are covered in teeth.

We are rippling with muscle.

We are sprouting hair.

We are producing liquids.

We can produce bodies.

We can produce whole worlds.

1: We've got walls of muscle.

2: We've got holes.

3: We've got deep, deep, deep holes.

1, 2, 3: We've got holes that could swallow you up.

1: We speak out of our holes.

We reject your definition of holes.

We reject your whole framework.

1: We've been pushed down into the ground.

We've been growing down there.

Spreading roots.

Sprouting shoots.

2: We're a rhizome.

3: We're many headed.

1: We're a mandrake root

2: Pulling ourselves out of the ground and

3: screaming.

1: We're harpies.

2: We're a three headed bitch.

3: We've been guarding the gates.

1, 2, 3: Now we're throwing them open.

1: Now we're a hydra

2: And you've run out of fire to burn us.

3: We are coming up from underground.

1, 2, 3: We're climbing out.

1: This is a take over. We're taking over.

You came here to look.

We're giving you something to watch.

We're looking right back.

We're not interested in looking good for you.

We've been pushed down.

Now we're pushing back.

You made the road one way

We're driving back.

This might be a bumpy ride.

Hold tight.

3: If I am happy with my body and the way it feels to shake my flesh and sing

1, 2: NO

3: If I am happy with my body and the way it feels to shake my flesh

1, 2: NO

3: If I am happy with my body and the way it feels

1, 2: NO

3: If I am happy with my body

1, 2: NO

3: If I am happy

1, 2: NO

3: If I am

1, 2: NO

1, 2, 3: Now we're saying no.

2: We can destroy.

3: We can crush.

2: We can flatten you with the palm of one hand.

3: We can turn your bones to stone with one look.

2: We can spin the thread of your life and we can cut if off.

3: We can sing a song to pull you in and crush your skull to pieces.

1: We can turn ourselves into a bird.

2: A fist.

3: a hand grenade.

1: We can see into the past.

2: The present.

3: The future.

1, 2, 3: We are a force of nature

And because we are a force of nature

We do not apologise.

We are explaining

if you're all about what's natural and unnatural

that it is unnatural for us to be kind to you

if you have made those among us feel like ripping off our bodies like a jacket

if you have made those among us seek out quiet places to scream.

1: We have all been forced.

2: And we all have mothers who have been forced.

3: And we all have sisters who have been forced.

1: They have been covering our mouths.

2: They have been flattening us.

3: They have been locking us up like a pack of dogs.

1: We have space at our table.

2: Fill it.

3: Or turn back.

1, 2, 3: Your choice.

[10 second silence to permit departure]

1, 2, 3: Some rules:

1: Do not try to reduce us.

2: Do not try to compress us.

3: Do not try to limit our curves.

1: We've been in the dark. Now our eyes are adjusting.

2: We've been laying foundations

3: We've been digging deep

1, 2, 3: Now we're ready to start.

1: We're making a space that's ours.

2: We're taking it for ourselves.

3: We're forming a ring around it.

1, 2, 3: Do not try and force yourselves inside that ring.

1: There will be consequences.

2: You have been warned.

3: Do not interrupt us.

1: And do not, under any circumstances

2: We repeat

1, 2, 3: DO NOT

INTERRUPT

OUR GRINDING.

MUSIC. DANCING MUSIC

THEY DANCE

SOME OF IT IS A COORDINATED ROUTINE

IMPROVISED ELEMENTS SHOULD BE INCORPORATED.

THERE SHOULD BE SWEATING

THEY START TO SING.

Now we're launching an attack
on the body of the whole
found the weapons to fight back
and we're filling up our bowls

Drill, baby, drill
drill, baby, drill
drill deep
We're making holes.

We're a deadly virus
We're eating up the cells
We're infecting what's around us
with these bodies with these smells

We are coming from the inside out
growing roots and shoots rhizome
many headed sprouting snouts
we multiply our own genome

We're building up our forces
and we're filling up the spaces
and we're opening our mouths
and we're going to fill our faces

Drill, baby, drill
drill, baby, drill
drill deep
We're making holes.

We've got muscles watch us flex
see these biceps see these pecs
see these sinews in our necks
we can hex don't make us vexed

So Drill, baby, drill
drill, baby, drill
drill deep
We're making holes.

We're getting bigger wider
We're filling up the stage
when we put this food inside us
We're fuelling the rage

We're splitting all the stitches
they're ripping at the seams
We're a baying band of bitches
and we're drinking all the cream.

THE SONG FINISHES.

1, 2, 3: We're going to tell you a story.

1: The story is about knowing.

2: The story is about blaming.

3: The story is about border control.

1, 2, 3: The story is about a woman.

1: The story is about a woman who wanted to know.

2: Because she wanted to know, she looked over the threshold.

3: Because she looked, they blamed her for the monsters.

1: First there was a man who stole resources.

2: First there was a man who stole.

3: First there was a man.

1, 2, 3: The gods found out about the man.

They found out that he stole their fire.

They punished him.

1: But the man became a hero of the people.

2: The fire that he'd stolen kept on burning.

3: The fire lit up the darkness.

1, 2, 3: So then they made a woman.

1: She was the first woman.

2: They made her out of dirt and gobs of spit.

3: They gave her gifts.

1: A gown

2: a crown

3: a mouth

1, 2, 3: and words for it to speak.

1: And then

2: a box.

3: A big black box.

1, 2, 3: Don't open the box.

1: They made the box with hinges.

2: They left the box unlocked.

3: She lifted the lid.

1, 2, 3: She looked.

1: They set a trap to force her into

2: so she'd be culpable.

3: She was punished

1, 2, 3: For being a punishment.

For crossing the threshold.

For opening the hatch.

1: They called her a curse.

2: If you create the curse

3: Don't be surprised to see it mirrored back at you.

1, 2, 3: Pandora.

THEY SING

She lifted up the latch
hell came screaming out the hatch
coughed up ghouls she couldn't catch
although she tried so hard to snatch

(Oooh, it was a bottomless box)

out from the box came darkness
out from the box came pain
out from the box came starkness
and a mighty hurricane

then from the box came snakes
then from the box came blood
then from the box came monsters
before she shut it with a thud

(Oooh, it was a bottomless box)

before the ticking of a clock
the people threw her in the dock:
she had opened up a box
which was a present from the boss.

(Oooh, it had been left unlocked)

They told her
get back in your box Pandora
get back in your box
get back in your box you lying thieving dirty pox.

(Oooh, they threw her in the stocks)

You brought our light to darkness
You brought sickness and cold
You're nothing but bad news
To the marrow of your soul.

They told her
get back in your box Pandora
get back in your box
get back in your box you lying thieving dirty pox.

(Oooh, it was a bottomless box)

SPOKEN/RAP:

She was kicked for being tricked
blamed for the trickery that tricked her.
blame the daughter for the slaughter
and you're surely in deep water.

It's the one who had the thought
to give the darkness as a gift
it's the one who made the lid
the kind of lid that you can lift
it's the mouths that made the fiction
into fact to cause the friction.
On that foul faction's depiction
we pronounce our maledictions.

They said get back in your box Pandora
get back in your box
get back in your box you lying thieving dirty pox.

SONG ENDS

1, 2, 3: The story isn't over.

1: They needed the box to be opened.

2: They needed Pandora to need to know

3: So they could blame her for it

1: shut her back inside it

2: And compress her

3: until she became the box.

1: Until people couldn't speak of her outside of it.

2: The box was welded to her name

3: and welded shut again.

1, 2, 3: But the darkness came before Pandora.

1: The darkness came before the box

2: The darkness came before the woman

3: and the man

1: and the monsters

2: and the looking

3: and the locks.

1, 2, 3: Now we're opening up the box.

1: Now we're coming up out of the darkness.

2: Now we're lifting up the latch.

3: Now we're bursting the locks.

1, 2, 3: Now we're blowing off the hinges

And we're coming like a hurricane.

The big black box blows itself open.

2 takes out a big black bag from inside.

1, 2, 3: Now we are telling you a story.

1: The story is about looking.

2: The story is about a monster.

3: The story is about a woman.

1: The story is about a woman who was too attractive to look at.

2: Because she was too attractive to look at, he couldn't help but force his way into her.

3: Because he forced his way into her, they turned her into a monster.

1: They turned her skin to scales

2: And her hair to snakes

3: And locked her up in a cave.

1, 2, 3: Medusa.

1: She was in the temple.

2: It was her hair he saw first.

3: It pulled him in.

1: He came close and told her to smile.

1, 2, 3: Then he raped her on the spot.

She was irresistible.

2: The priestesses found her in a heap

3: They told the goddess

1: The goddess was angry

2: The goddess exacted her punishment on the woman.

3: For the sin of having golden hair in a temple

1: For the sin of being seen by a man

2: she had snakes sprout from her scalp

3: and was de-faced.

1: Because she looked too attractive she was deformed.

2: Because of her deformity she was compressed.

3: From her compression

1, 2, 3: she distilled the power to kill.

To suck life out through a pair of eyes.

To murder anyone who looked.

1: Rumours ran wild

2: about this new face like a

3: slit gut

1, 2, 3: like a

1: pulped eye

1, 2, 3: like a

2: saw cutting teeth

1, 2, 3: ugliness itself.

1: But ugliness is made by the one who's looking.

2: And Medusa couldn't be seen.

3: The act of the look stopped the looker stone still on the spot.

1: The act of the look made the looker into a

2: sculpture to

3: admire.

1: People kept their distance

2: respected her space

3: feared her presence

1: until he came with a curved mirror

1, 2, 3: chopped her head off

2: shoved it in a bag

3: for a wedding gift.

1: She spurted blood that bubbled black.

2: She sprouted.

3: From her sawn neck leapt a winged horse and a giant with a golden sword.

1, 2, 3: Her sisters screamed.

He scarpered.

1: She was our sister.

2: We were her witness.

3: We were there.

1: She must be here now

2: Because you're looking petrified.

3: We're looking for revenge.

Something is moving in the second Big Woman's big black bag.

Blood starts to leak from it.

A hissing noise. From inside.

1: Her blood stained the sea red. Shot forth coral.

2: Her blood dripped snakes onto the Saharan sand.

The blood is trickling towards the feet of the audience in rivulets. The hissing is getting louder.

3: Her cut head scorched sea monsters still

1: And stopped a palace full of people in their tracks.

Squelching sounds, gristly popping noises.

2: He slunk in like a dog in the shadows

3: caught her in a trick of the light

1: and carved her like a turkey.

1, 2, 3: It's enough to make you lose your self-control.

Blood. More blood.

A strangled hissing gurgling bubbling foaming muffled scream from the bag

The second Big Woman opens the bag

The sound gets louder

The second Big Woman reaches her hand in

The hand grips

BOOM.

Light cuts out.

FLASH OF LIGHT

dazzling

Light cuts out.

FLASH OF LIGHT

trapped in a held mirror and dazzling

hissing gurgling crunching slithering

a beat from below beneath the speech spoken

2: Looking is an act.

Things know when you're looking.

Some things don't like to be looked at.

Even sub-atomic particles know when you're watching them.

A single tiny point of light

When you try to measure them they split themselves and scatter.

Try to track the path of a particle

Point of light hits the mirror and sprays across the space into bands of sharp stars.

And it acts like a wave that can't be caught.

Try to track the action of that wave

single point of light once more

And it becomes a single point.

If you try to reduce it

1, 2, 3: It will multiply.

lights crawling across the audience space moving like ants or bees or spiders

2: If you try to trap it

1, 2, 3: It will scatter.

2: The act of observation alters the outcome of the experiment.

Elementary particles don't like being watched.

The fabric of the universe will not be caught.

So if you ask us what's the harm in looking

We tell you it's in our nature to resist capture.

It's in our nature to evade your grasp.

We don't like being watched

If we don't want to be seen.

But when we want you to see us

You cannot look away.

LIGHT SPRINGS ON

BLOOD EVERYWHERE

THE THREE BIG WOMEN SPROUT WINGS

The hissing is louder still

A suppressed scream takes shape as sound, tethered:

3: We are capable of monstrosities.

We can cut out your tongue

And nail it to the walls.

We can hound you til you run mad.

We can rip your skin with our teeth.

We can scratch until there are holes where your eyes are.

We have sharpened our nails

We are ready to attack

We are ready to attack you like a pack of dogs

1, 2, 3: [BARKING]

[BARKING]

[BARKING]

blood drips from the ceiling

3: Don't tempt us to do that to you.

If we are under the influence

If our blood is drunk with rage

If in this rage we tear flesh

If in this drunken rage we bite and suck the blood

If in this drunken rage we feed upon your blood
until we are full

If in this drunken rage we happen to detach your hip
from your pelvis

and sink in our teeth

and feed

1, 2, 3: we can't be held responsible.

We're here for justice.

It's not our fault.

3: It is your fault if you try to deform us.

It is your fault if you try to make us attractive.

It is your fault if you try to stop us.

If you try that, we will end you.

We will eat you alive. We mean literally.

We will open ourselves wide

and leak enough liquid to drown you.

We will sprout hair from every follicle

wrap it round your neck

and squeeze.

We will reach our hands out

push them down your throats

And bed our fists in your guts.

And then we will pull.

We will pull everything out from inside of you.

We will unravel you.

And then we will start to eat.

We will feed on you.

Feels like the room is full of things with wings and scales

We will open our mouths wide

We will pull your insides into our insides

and we will digest you.

We will fatten ourselves on your body

until we are massive.

We will take all of you inside us.

Every inch.

We will make cells out of your meat.

We will grow wider and wider and wider.

We will take up more and more and more space.

The more you try to stop us, the more space we will take up.

The more you try to push into us, the less of yourself
you will have left.

We can't be held responsible if you're screaming no

And in this moment our bodies overpower us.

We can't be stopped when our blood is up.

Once the teeth have sunk in we have no way of detaching our jaws.

It's not our problem. It's just biology.

We are not accountable if you try to drive us mad.

And you have been driving us mad.

And we are ready to feed.

The sharp star shapes twinkle.

A moment of eerie calm, then near-kindness that flows through their words.

2: But we're not greedy.

We believe in sharing.

1: We share an eye.

2: We share a tongue.

3: We pass them round.

2: We've learnt to do that through necessity.

We've learnt to work with our resources.

We've had to learn to shift our shapes

Make muteness mutable

And transform silence into a song.

1: We are capable of the keenest kindness

2: We can be infinitely gentle

1: We can be softer than a summer breeze

3: But we have had to learn to use our fists

2: And punch harder than a heavyweight champion.

3: So naturally we're feeling violent.

1, 2, 3: You try being buried in a hole
for two hundred thousand years

and then come back to us.

2: Something happens

1: A process of distillation

2: A series of compressions

3: A deformation of matter

1: A hardening under pressure

2: Becoming dense

3: uncrackable

1: intractible

2: unliftable

3: unshiftable

1: insurmountable

2: irreducible

3: a crucible

1: of unflinching

2: unblinking

3: undiluted

1, 2, 3: force.

2 makes a strange, deep sound.

3: What's happening?

1: Hold tight.

3: Shouldn't cage an animal

1: Then put fingers through the bars.

1, 3: Confinement multiplies the pressure.

The pressure of the

2: threat.

A huge force is building.

1: You're –

2: – tense – – tensed

3: been pushed hard

2: this is dangerous

A siren sounds

3: What's happening?

1: Hold tight.

2: Feel it ripping

3: Feeling hungry

1: Hold tight.

3: Who's pulling?

2: You are.

1: We are.

2, 3: Deforming

1, 2, 3: WE ARE

2: pulling in

1: pulling everything in

1, 3: No direction left

1, 2: only In

3: into the

1, 2, 3: HOLE

1: No rules

3: to describe this

1: To see

2, 3: you have to cross the boundary

1: the event horizon

2: but –

3: do that and you're

1: done for

2: no escape

1: no turning back

2: You

1, 2: drew the lines

2, 3: applied the pressure

1, 2, 3: compressed

2, 3: reduced

1: til we were nothing but a

1 ,2, 3: HOLE

2: now we're taking

3: you

1: into the

1, 2, 3: HOLE

2: making

1, 3: you

1: the

1, 2, 3: HOLE

WE ARE

3: becoming more attractive

1, 2, 3: WE ARE

2: gaining mass

1: getting

1, 2, 3: MASSIVE

1, 2: getting stellar–

1, 2, 3: – MASSIVE

SUPER MASSIVE

3: growing curves

2: big big curves

2: Yes

2, 3: spacetime curves

1, 2, 3: WE ARE

2: irresistibly attractive

3: Yes

1: gravitationally

3: irresistible

2: pulling so hard

1: even light can't escape

2, 3: Yes

3: magnetic

1, 2: electromagnetic

1: absorbing

3: absorbing electromagnetic radiation

2: blackbody

1, 2, 3: Yes

1: radiating

1, 3: blackbody radiation

2: seeping blackbody radiation

1, 2, 3: Yes

1, 2: disrupting binary systems

3: sucking in binary solar systems

3: no way back

2: this might be a pathway

3: it might be a

1, 2, 3: MASSIVE BLACK

3: bottomless pit.

1: Been

2: smashed

1: so we'll

2: smash

3: Yes

1: been

2: compressed

1: so we'll

2, 3: destroy

1, 3: Yes

1: been

1, 2, 3: pushed

1: so we'll

1, 2, 3: pull

1: A singularity.

1, 2: WE ARE

3: deforming the theory of relativity

1, 2, 3: WE ARE

2: transforming attraction

1, 2, 3: WE ARE

2, 3: a singularity

1, 2: a collective singularity

1, 2, 3: HOLE

1: approaching infinite density

Siren sounds louder spins faster overlaps itself.

1, 2, 3: HOLE

2: Too late.

3: You looked.

1, 2, 3: A HOLE

1: Pulling harder and harder and harder

1, 2, 3: A MASSIVE HOLE

2: Pulling in entire star systems

1, 2, 3: A SUPER MASSIVE HOLE

3: Compressing them into darkness

1, 2, 3: WE ARE A SUPERMASSIVE BLACK HOLE.

THE SONG BEGINS

This is our
BLACKBODY RADIATION
WE'RE YOUR FUTURE HOLOGRAPHIC SCREENS
WE'RE LINKING UP. WE'RE FORMING ONE
WE'RE A SUPERMASSIVE BLACK HOLE, QUEEN.

All the holes are joining up
Into one enormous mass
Now you are at the centre
And there's no way you can pass

We're talking theories of relativity
We're talking about what you think you see
We're talking about how to be
When you make us enemies
Now we're infinite in density

BLACKBODY RADIATION
CROSSED THE EVENT HORIZON NOW YOU SEE
THIS IS THE SINGULARITY
WE'RE A SUPERMASSIVE BLACK HOLE, QUEEN.

particle-	antiparticle
gravity	and the way it pulls
pronouns and	def'nite articles
all of this	rather farcical
why did you	ever start this all
you will be destroyed	unavoidable

BLACKBODY RADIATION
WE'RE YOUR FUTURE HOLOGRAPHIC SCREENS
WE'RE LINKING UP. WE'RE FORMING ONE
WE'RE A SUPERMASSIVE BLACK HOLE, QUEEN.

If you like it then you shouldn't put a ring around it
You tried to classify our insides but we won't allow it
We break the laws: the mechanism's been confounded
If you're looking for annihilation then you've found it

BLACKBODY RADIATION
CROSSED THE EVENT HORIZON NOW YOU SEE
THIS IS THE SINGULARITY
WE'RE A SUPERMASSIVE BLACK HOLE, QUEEN.

The rhythm starts to shift, skip, warp, bend, menace

47

BLACKBODY RADIATION
WE'RE YOUR FUTURE HOLOGRAPHIC SCREENS
WE'RE LINKING UP. WE'RE FORMING ONE
WE'RE A SUPERMASSIVE BLACK HOLE, QUEEN.

1: Hold tight.

The rhythm skips and skitters underneath the words: cut-up parts of the chorus return in snatches.

| SSSSSSUPERMASSIVE   BLACK HOLE, |

2: Hold tight.

| SSSSSS – |

3: No way back.

1: Black hole.

3: Hold tight.

|SSSSSS| | O O O O |

2, 3: No way back.

2: Black hole.

1, 2, 3: Hold tight.

1, 2: No way back.

3: Black hole.

The stars spiral downwards towards the hole in the ground

the phrase plays back in reverse

thgit dloH

1: Hole.

faster and faster

2: Hole.

3: Hole.

2, 1: Hole.

2: Hole.

1, 2: Hole.

2, 3: Hole.

3: Hole.

2: Hole.

1, 2, 3: Hole.

A BURST

THE LIGHT OF A MILLION SUNS

SUCKED INTO THE BLACK BOX

DOWN THE HATCH

THE HATCH SLAMS SHUT.

nothing.

darkness.

silence.

still.

Still,

still.

Tick.

Tick.

Tick. Tock.

Tick Tick.

A metronome swings backwards and forwards in the dark.
Irregular.

Tock.

Tock.

Tick.

Tick.

Just the sound of the metronome.
Then speech from the darkness.
Delineated as below. Spoken in order.
Pronounced at random by five voices.
Speakers can take any number
of consecutive lines and speak over
or around each other.
If sounds bang into each other:
even better. That's life.

– now

– at

– the

– bottom of

– everything

– still

– something

– moving

– here

– yes

– listen

– there

– a particle

– a grain of

– what

– an ingrained

– tiny smallest

– something

– coming

– from the

– nothing

– if you could look

– you would dislodge it

– this is what you can't examine

– this is the darkest

– of the darknesses

– no way of

– knowing

– how it happens

– til it

– happens

– can't predict with

– certainty

– can't trap or

– see inside the

– darkness

– where the question is not

– what is it

– more like how likely

– how like this

– thing

– would it

– be to do this

– thing

– that acts

– according to

– chance

– tending towards a

– cloud

– of

– prob

– a

– bil

– i

– ty

– not

– infinity

– not

– logic

– this is the force

– that underpins

– the universe

– a chance

– a probability

– a galaxy

– boiled down to a

– single point of

– information

– compressed

– below the scale of

– certainty

– into

– darkness

> *A light begins to flash on and off briefly at random intervals across the stage, falling upon body parts we can't attach to bodies*

– then

– a speck

– swings back

– out of the dark

– spits out itself

– and winds itself into

– a rope

– a track

– it wants to

– cluster and

– gain force

– into a

– swarm of

– particles

– a chain of

– thought

– words cluster to the thought

– fists cluster to the words

– worlds cluster to the fists

– the worlds collide

– the universe is building

– something from nothing

– at every moment

– collision

– of the smallest grains of mass

– smashed

– at every moment from

– nothing

– flip

– into

– something

– a pair of particles bang themselves into being

– something out of nothing

– pulling the

– rabbit

– out of the

– hole

– that swallows it –

Now the below is spoken by a voice or voices coming from several directions at once through the darkness as the light continues to flash up and down at shorter intervals:

Listen   I am talking   I am opening my mouth
  I want to be at the beginning again   to the time before it
all happened   after it was all over   but time isn't anything
only exists insomuch as we experience it   in a sequence of
warming and cooling   a direction of heat   an exchange
of heat but heat scorches   I've got the burns to
prove it   time bends words into things which slice
  I can show you the scars   they told me things aren't
anything   things are only other things smashing into each
other   but I feel like a thing that exists   spat
up and scattered over time   smashing and being smashed
    pendulum knocked into motion   pushing back
    I've been smashed and I've smashed and smashed
and smashed and smashed   and smashed and smashed and
smashed and   smashed and smashed   every part of me
a combination of smashing things and things being smashed
  I am smashing these words into a hole   ripping
myself a new mouth   I am smashing the glass and spilling
the words all over you into your body vibrating you with
my frequency   making something out of nothing   I am
energy   I'm tired   I am capable   I matter
I am matter   See how I carry myself see how I scatter
see how I shatter   I was a child   I remember   the dark
  before they made me fear it   wet and warm   then

57

One by one, from the darkness, sharp stars start to cover the space again

stars stuck to my wall   sharp stars that glowed in the
dark   sharp stars that dug under my fingernails   when I tried
to pull them off they made me bleed   heart smashing blood
through my body   I want to be sluiced   I want to be clean
  clean myself of all my organs   grow new ones   smash myself
out of myself   spit myself out   I am trying to find
the opening   I am hoping   this time it will be different
I want to find new colours   I want to feel I'm not filled in yet
    I want to be gentle   I am losing time   . I'm tired   I have
to move

listen   I am talking   I need it pushed through the holes
where your ears are I need it pushed across the gaps between your
synapses –

The metronome ticks faster and faster, with increasing regularity

I –

      TICK   *TOCK*   *TICK*   *TOCK*

I need –

        TICK   *TOCK* *TICK*   *TOCK*

I need you –

          TICKTOCKTICKTOCK

l need you to –

      LIGHT UP ON EVERYTHING AND ALL OF US.

      THE METRONOME STOPS.

I need you to listen.